C000304132

Newman

His Life and Legacy

by
Fr Ian Ker

*All booklets are published thanks to the
generous support of the members of the
Catholic Truth Society*

CATHOLIC TRUTH SOCIETY
PUBLISHERS TO THE HOLY SEE

Contents

The Anglican years 3

The path to Rome 19

The Catholic years 31

Beatification 55

The Anglican years

John Henry Newman (1801–1890) was born on 21 February 1801 at 80 Old Broad Street in the City of London. His father, John Newman, was a banker, the son of a London grocer, who originally came from Cambridgeshire. His mother, Jemima, was the daughter of Henry Fourdrinier, a paper maker, whose family were originally French Huguenot refugees. They had married in 1799 and John Henry was their first child of six.

Formative years

In 1803 the family moved to 17 Southampton Street (later Southampton Place), Bloomsbury. They were sufficiently well off to own another Georgian house, in the country— Grey Court House near Ham Common, Surrey. In 1808 Newman was sent to Ealing School, a well-known private boarding-school. Saved from the ordeals of a public school—he managed later to avoid being sent to Winchester—he enjoyed school life. Apart from his academic studies (in which he excelled) and games (in which he had no interest), he acted in Latin plays, played the violin, won prizes for speeches, and edited periodicals, in which he wrote articles in the style of

Addison. This happy childhood came to an abrupt end in March 1816 when the financial collapse after the Napoleonic wars forced his father's bank to close. While his father tried unsuccessfully to manage a brewery at Alton, Hampshire, Newman stayed on at school through the summer holidays because of the family crisis.

The period from the beginning of August to 21 December 1816, when the next term ended, Newman always regarded as the turning point of his life. Alone at school and shocked by the family disaster, he fell ill in August. Later he came to see it as one of the three great providential illnesses of his life, for it was in the autumn of 1816 that he underwent a religious conversion under the influence of one of the schoolmasters, the Revd Walter Mayers, who had himself shortly before been converted to a Calvinistic form of evangelicalism. Newman had had a conventional upbringing in an ordinary Church of England home, where the emphasis was on the Bible rather than dogmas or sacraments, and where any sort of evangelical 'enthusiasm' would have been frowned upon. In fact, his conversion lacked the kind of emotional upheaval associated with evangelicalism, although the theology he learned from Mayers and the books Mayers lent him were certainly Calvinistic: he believed he was 'elected to eternal glory' (Newman, *Apologia*). However, it was not the Calvinism (which he was to abandon) that was important, but the fact that the dogmas of Christianity, particularly the Trinity, now became real to him in a way that they had not been before. Of the evangelical authors recommended by Mayers, the most important was the biblical commentator Thomas Scott, whose autobiography, *The Force of Truth* (1779), recounted his conversion from Unitarianism to Trinitarian Christianity. The other critical influence was Joseph Milner's *History of the Church of Christ* (1794–1809), which contained long extracts from the church fathers; Newman was thrilled by the picture they presented of the early church. At the same time, however, he read Thomas Newton's *Dissertation on the Prophecies* (1754–8), a book that convinced him that the pope must be the Antichrist predicted in scripture. On the personal level, the effect of his conversion was that he felt that God was calling him to the kind of sacrificial service, such as missionary work, that would involve celibacy: 'it would be the will of God that I should lead a single life' (Newman, *Apologia*).

In 1817 Newman entered Trinity College, Oxford, when he was still only sixteen. In May 1818 he won a college scholarship. His first published writing was an anti-Catholic verse romance, *St Bartholomew's Eve* (1818), which he wrote with his close college friend John William Bowden. His final examinations in 1820 were an unexpected disaster, failing as he did altogether in mathematics and achieving only a fourth (the lowest class) in classics. He had been expected to get a double first but he was exhausted through overwork. Since his scholarship was for nine years, he was able to return to Oxford, and on 12 April 1822 he was elected to a fellowship by examination at Oriel, a college which prided itself on its ability to discern academic potential.

Fellow of Oriel

Newman's evangelical views soon began to be undermined by the liberal atmosphere of the Oriel common room, which was famous for its 'Noetics' such as Thomas Arnold who believed in the primacy of reason in theology. Among them was Richard Whately, whose famous *Elements of Logic* (1826) Newman helped to compose, and whose importance in teaching him to think for himself Newman later recognized. However, he was still sufficiently under the influence of Mayers to decide to take holy orders while still teaching, and in 1824 he was ordained deacon (and a year later priest) and appointed curate at St Clement's, a working-class parish in east Oxford. Throwing himself energetically into pastoral work, he came to believe that the standard evangelical distinction between 'nominal' and 'real' Christians did not work in practice. This realization seemed to be supported by the fact that St Paul had not divided Christians into the converted and the unconverted, an observation Newman owed to another of the Noetics, Edward Hawkins, who stressed that tradition was needed as well as scripture. He also began to abandon the doctrine of imputed righteousness in favour of that of baptismal regeneration, the rejection of which was seen as marking out the true evangelical.

Whately was responsible for Newman's first serious publication, an article in 1824 for the *Encyclopaedia metropolitana* on Cicero, who clearly influenced Newman's rhetorical style as a controversialist. A further two articles in the *Encyclopaedia*, on Apollonius of Tyana and miracles in the Bible, followed in 1826. In spite of the shyness that affected him all his life, Newman had begun to come out of his shell at Oriel. In 1825 Whately became principal of the tiny, run-down Alban Hall and invited Newman to become vice-principal. One important result of this close collaboration was Whately's impressing on Newman's mind the idea of the church as a divine body separate from the state. But in 1826 he resigned both this post and his curacy on being appointed a tutor at Oriel.

Newman later wrote that the influences leading him in a religiously liberal direction were abruptly checked by his suffering first, at the end of 1827, a kind of nervous collapse brought on by overwork and family financial troubles, and then, at the beginning of 1828, the bereavement of his beloved youngest sister, Mary, who died suddenly. There was also a crucial theological factor:

his fascination since 1816 with the fathers of the church, whose works he began to read systematically in the long vacation of 1828.

Ironically, but not altogether surprisingly, Newman had supported his mentor, Edward Hawkins, in his successful candidature for the vacant Oriel provostship at the beginning of 1828 against the high-church John Keble, whom he hardly knew. One consequence was that Newman now succeeded Hawkins as vicar of the university church of St Mary's. At first Hawkins supported Newman in his role as a reforming tutor, determined to raise both the religious tone of the college and also its academic standards. But the volte-face by the Tory government in granting Catholic emancipation in 1829 led to a sharp division between Hawkins, who supported this liberal measure and therefore the re-election of Sir Robert Peel as MP for the Anglican university, and Newman, who was part of the successful opposition to what was seen as treachery on the part of the political party of the established church. The Peel affair coincided with a new tutorial system drawn up by Newman with the collaboration of his colleagues Richard Hurrell Froude and Robert Isaac Wilberforce. Its purpose was to strengthen the academic and pastoral relationship between the undergraduate and his individual tutor. But Hawkins strongly disapproved of the attempt to change the role of the tutor from that of a lecturer with responsibility for discipline to that of a personal moral tutor, and in 1830 informed Newman that no further students would be sent to him.

Freedom from teaching duties meant that Newman had no difficulty in accepting a commission in 1831 to write a history of church councils. Instead, he ended up by writing *The Arians of the Fourth Century* (1833). As a work of historical theology, it reflects Newman's own reaction against the religious liberalism of the day. But while insisting on the necessity of dogmatic formulations, Newman was also careful to acknowledge the inadequacy of human language to express the mysteries of faith—an awareness which stemmed from his discovery of the early church's principle of 'economy', which also had a practical application in the way in which Christianity was taught. This economical method of imparting truths was connected with the primitive practice of 'reserve', which, Newman pointed out, was the reverse of the current evangelical preaching of the atonement to arouse feelings that would lead to conversion. This reticence in the face of transcendent mystery was to become a hallmark of Tractarianism.

On 8 December 1832 Newman set sail from Falmouth for the Mediterranean with Richard Hurrell Froude, who was going abroad for his health, and his father. Because of an outbreak of cholera, the first place they were able to visit properly was Corfu, where Newman tried to find out what he could about the Orthodox Church. He was disconcerted to find how like the Roman Catholic Church it was in its veneration of Mary and the saints and its liturgical ceremonies. Even more disconcerting was Rome, where they arrived in March 1833: here was the 'eternal' city of the apostles, martyrs, and saints, from where the gospel had come to England; but this same city which so impressed and moved Newman, and where there seemed so much to admire in the devotions and piety of the people, was also, so he still believed, the city of a corrupt and superstitious religion. All this time his thoughts were never far from home, where the Reform Bill, which threatened the position of the established church, had been passed in 1832, and where the Irish Church Reform Bill, which threatened to suppress ten sees of the church in Ireland, was before parliament. In March he sent off the first poems he and Froude were writing for a regular verse section, to be called (and in 1836 published as) 'Lyra apostolica', in the *British Magazine*, a review recently started by Hugh James Rose, a Cambridge high-churchman, in defence of the church.

Instead of accompanying the Froudes home in April, Newman decided to revisit Sicily, where he fell seriously ill of gastric or typhoid fever. Many were dying from the epidemic, but Newman was confident that he would live: 'God has still work for me to do' (Newman, *Autobiographical Writings*). When he came later to write a graphic account of his fever, he looked back on it as the third of the three pivotal illnesses in these formative years. On his way home, while at sea, he wrote 'Lead, kindly light', which, with its mood of thanksgiving and trust, has become a famous hymn. He arrived back in Oxford on 9 July 1833. Five days later Keble preached the assize sermon from the pulpit of the university church, published as *National Apostasy*, protesting against state interference in the Church of England. Newman always regarded that day as the beginning of the Oxford or Tractarian Movement.

The Tracts

If the 'Lyra apostolica', which began appearing in June 1833, were the first literary productions of the Oxford Movement, the next were a series of papers by Newman, later published as *The Church of the Fathers* (1840), which he began sending in August 1833 to the *British Magazine*. The first, which appeared in October 1833, pointed out that the early Christian church had depended not on the state but on the people. It was preceded by the publication on 9 September 1833 of Tract 1 (*Ad clerum*) of the Tracts for the Times, which was on the doctrine of the apostolic succession and was anonymously written by Newman. The Tracts were his idea, and he insisted on publishing them himself rather than allowing a board to authorize and supervise their publication, since 'living movements do not come of committees' (Newman, *Apologia*). Indeed, Newman was against any kind of formal association to organize the movement, because it would involve compromises and inhibit individual action, preferring to build up a network of personal contacts among sympathizers throughout the country, particularly through the circulation of the Tracts. These soon aroused furious controversy, were increasingly in demand, and began to attract new writers, including the regius professor of Hebrew, Edward Bouverie Pusey. Accusations of exaggeration and extremism did not surprise Newman: an element of excess, he thought, was an inevitable part of fighting for a true cause, in this case the protection of the church against state encroachment and the preservation of the apostolic faith against such liberal plans of reform as Thomas Arnold's proposal to make the Church of England more doctrinally comprehensive in order to avert the threat of disestablishment.

In March 1834 the first volume of Newman's *Parochial Sermons* was published (the whole series appeared from 1834 to 1842, reprinted in 1868 as the first six volumes of *Parochial and Plain Sermons*). As well as being one of the great classics of Christian spirituality, the pastoral sermons he preached in St Mary's were almost as central to the Oxford Movement as the Tracts. Unlike the latter, they deliberately avoided controversial issues, although the theology that underlay Newman's preaching was clearly influenced by his reading of the Greek fathers, as can be seen in the emphasis on the incarnation and the resurrection, the indwelling of the Holy Spirit and the sacraments, and the sense of the mystery of the Christian revelation. However, the profound influence they exerted at the time lay in their call to holiness, a call which could not be dissociated from the charisma of the preacher himself, who avoided all the usual oratorical devices of the pulpit but whose rapt intensity and low, soft, but strangely thrilling voice left unforgettable memories with many of his listeners. J. C. Shairp recalled: 'He laid his finger—how gently, yet how powerfully!—on some inner place in the hearer's heart, and told him things about himself he had never known till then' (J. C. Shairp, *Studies in Poetry and Philosophy*, 1868).

The *via media*

The most obvious criticism of the Tracts was that they were undermining the protestant character of the Church of England. In answer, Newman wrote two Tracts in 1834 to the effect that the English church was 'reformed' but also Catholic, occupying a *via media* or middle position between protestantism and Roman Catholicism. He welcomed, therefore, the chance to develop this view of the Anglican *via media* in October, when he was asked by one of the contributors to the Tracts to take over a theological debate he was having with a French priest called Jean-Nicolas Jager in the pages of *L'Univers* newspaper. Newman sent one lengthy letter translated into French before Christmas and the first part of a second letter in July 1835, but the controversy came to an end and the second part was never published. However, Newman was able to make use of the correspondence when he came to formulate his statement of the Anglican *via media* in the *Lectures on the prophetical office of the church, viewed relatively to Romanism and popular protestantism* (1837), which were delivered in 1836 in St Mary's. While admitting that Anglo-Catholicism was as yet more of an unrealized theory than a reality, he argued that it approximated far more closely to primitive Christianity than either protestantism, which neglected the church referred to in the creed, or Roman Catholicism, which substituted the authority of the church for that of the testimony of antiquity.

Concerned as he was with the urgent need to show that Tractarianism was not the same as Roman Catholicism, Newman also continued to battle against theological liberalism. In 1835 he published Tract 73, later republished as *On the Introduction of Rationalistic Principles into Revealed Religion*. He blamed evangelicalism for the subjectivity of modern religion, and explained Schleiermacher's theology as an attempt to justify intellectually a religion of feelings. He dated the beginning of open hostility between the Tractarians and the liberals to a sharp exchange he had with R. D. Hampden at the end of 1834 over an (unsuccessful) bill to remove the obligation to subscribe to the Thirty-Nine Articles at Oxford and Cambridge. It was, however, embarrassing for a Tractarian to have to insist on the articles, which were seen as the protestant title deeds of the established church, as the means of protecting the Anglican, and indeed religious, character of the university. Hampden had been appointed in 1832 to one of the vacant Oriel tutorships after the enforced resignation of Newman and his colleagues; then in March 1834 he had been elected to the chair of moral philosophy, for which Newman had also applied, not with any enthusiasm but because he thought the position might help the Tractarian cause. Much more serious was the appointment of Hampden in February 1836 as regius professor of divinity. A few days later Newman brought out a pamphlet, *Elucidations of Dr Hampden's Theological Statements*, attacking Hampden's liberal theology.

As vicar of St Mary's, Newman was in a position to put Tractarian principles into practice: he had begun daily morning prayer in church in 1834, as well as an evening service once a week, and after Easter 1837 he began an early communion service on Sundays. He had privately been using the Roman breviary for more than a year, having chosen Hurrell Froude's own copy from his books as a memento of his beloved friend, who had died after a long illness in 1836. Froude's papers were entrusted to Newman and Keble, and it was decided to begin by publishing his 'Private thoughts', which, Newman thought, revealed the kind of heroic saintly figure that the movement needed for a model, although he was afraid that the details of Froude's fasting and the very un-evangelical nature of his religious journal would increase the fear that the Tractarians were really crypto-papists.

Newman's second major attempt to establish an Anglican *via media* came with his *Lectures on Justification*, delivered in 1837 and published in 1838. He wanted to show that both the protestant theory of justification by faith alone and the Roman Catholic doctrine of justification by works were incomplete truths. The way through this apparently impassable Reformation controversy lay, for Newman, in the Johannine and Pauline doctrine of the indwelling of the Holy Spirit, who both justifies and sanctifies. Newman has been criticized for misrepresenting Luther, who was ostensibly his chief target, but the lectures remained a formidable indictment of popular evangelicalism, with its preoccupation with conversion and faith. Polemical as it was, the book—considered by some to be Newman's most brilliant theological work—was certainly a pioneering model of ecumenical theology in its resolution of a historic controversy by changing the terms of reference and setting the problem in a wholly new perspective.

In the summer term of 1838 Newman gave another series of lectures in the Adam de Brome Chapel at St Mary's entitled 'Lectures on the scripture proof of the doctrines of the church', most of which were published as Tract 85. The Anglican or *via media* position was that the creed is to be found not on the face of, or literally in, scripture, as protestant evangelicals claimed, but implicitly in it. This contrasted with the Roman Catholic view that tradition provides another source of revelation. The only other possibility was the liberal protestant denial that Christianity has an objectively ascertainable creed or doctrine. The lectures contain some of Newman's most brilliant biblical criticism, particularly in regard to the literary form of scripture.

As Newman had feared, the publication of the first two volumes of Froude's *Remains* in February 1838 had caused a stir, and even some alarm, among the less adventurous of the Tractarian supporters. As a result, a project to translate the Roman breviary, in which he was involved, was dropped. Meanwhile, opponents of the Tractarians decided to launch an appeal for the erection of a monument in Oxford to the protestant martyrs Cranmer, Ridley, and Latimer, as a kind of test of the loyalty of Newman and others to the Church of England. Newman, who refused to acknowledge them as representative of Anglicanism, had no intention of subscribing. In spite of, or because of, all the controversy and criticism, Newman had never felt more confident about the Tractarian cause. The Tracts had become best-sellers. He himself had taken on the editorship of the *British Critic* in January 1838, with the idea of its becoming the organ of the Tractarians. There, in the spring of 1839, at what he was to recall as the high point of the movement, he published an article, 'The state of religious parties'. After asserting that the Oxford Movement should be seen as part of the Romantic movement (in which Newman's favourite novelist Walter Scott was especially singled out) or a larger spiritual awakening after the rationalism of the eighteenth century, he argued that while liberalism was too cold to appeal and evangelicalism too inconsistent and unreal to convince, there existed an alternative to unbelief on the one hand and Roman Catholicism on the other, namely the *via media* of Anglo-Catholicism.

The path to Rome

Doubts about the Church of England and Tract 90

It was only three or four months later, in the summer vacation of 1839, that the first real doubt about the Anglican position assailed Newman. He had returned to his study of the early church and was rereading the history of the Monophysite heresy, when quite suddenly he was struck by the way in which at the Council of Chalcedon the pope had upheld the Catholic orthodox faith while the heretics had divided into an extreme and a more moderate party. What impressed him was the similarity to the current situation, with Rome on one side, protestantism on the other, and Anglicanism in the middle. Then in September his attention was drawn by a friend to an article in the *Dublin Review* by Nicholas Wiseman, the rector of the English College in Rome, on the Donatist schism in the African church, but with special reference to the Anglican claim. He was struck forcefully by the maxim of St Augustine quoted in the article: 'Securus judicat orbis terrarum' ('the verdict of the whole world is conclusive') . The principle that 'the deliberate judgment, in which the whole Church at length rests and acquiesces, is an infallible prescription and a final sentence against such portions of it as protest and secede' (Newman, *Apologia*) not only seemed to offer the key to understanding the whole course of ecclesiastical history but also to destroy the theory of the *via media*. The excitement of the moment passed away, but Newman's confidence in the notion of an Anglican *via media* was gone for ever. However, his objection to the doctrinal accretions of Rome remained, as well as his deep-seated antipathy to popery dating back to his evangelical conversion, which still had a strong emotional, although no longer intellectual, hold on him.

In February 1841 Newman wrote his first sustained work of satire, a series of letters to *The Times* entitled 'The Tamworth reading room', a riposte to a speech by Sir Robert Peel on the replacement of religion by education and knowledge as the moral basis of a new pluralist society. In his bitingly sarcastic defence of faith as the foundation of individual and social morality, Newman anticipated some of the central themes of his later educational and philosophical writings.

Since 1839 Newman had been worried not only about his own belief in Anglicanism but also about the difficulty of preventing younger Tractarians from leaving a church in which the devotions and externals of a more developed Anglo-Catholicism had not yet come into being for the Church of Rome, which offered what they saw as the fullness of both Catholic doctrine and devotion. The crucial problem posed by the apparently protestant Thirty-Nine Articles led to Newman's publishing his highly contentious Tract 90 on 27 February 1841 which demonstrated, sometimes with what were considered by some to be intellectual sleights of hand, how the articles of the Anglican church were 'patient of a Catholic interpretation'. He argued, some protestants believed disingenuously, that the articles were not intended to exclude those Anglicans of Catholic sympathies but to protest against the errors of so-called popery. On 16 March the vice-chancellor, heads of colleges, and proctors issued a public censure—only a few hours before Newman's *A Letter Addressed to the Rev R. W. Jelf* appeared in his defence. In it he condemned the popular religion of popery, while at the same time comparing it to the kind of popular protestantism that existed in what he argued was the essentially Catholic Church of England. However, he agreed to a demand by his bishop, Richard Bagot, bishop of Oxford, that no further Tracts should be published.

In the summer vacation of 1841, as in 1839, Newman put aside controversy to return to his patristic studies, and again was assailed by doubts about the Anglican position. This time it was the Arian heresy—he was busy translating St Athanasius for the Library of the Fathers, a project he and Pusey had begun planning in 1836—which presented a disturbing parallel to the contemporary situation. Again, there were the same divisions: the extreme Arians, the semi-Arians, and Rome; again the truth lay not with the *via media* but with Rome. This was the first of the three blows that, Newman was later to say, finally broke him. The second was the series of condemnations of Tract 90 that the bishops began issuing. The third was the agreement, which became law in 1841, between the Prussian and English governments to set up a bishopric in Jerusalem that would alternate between an Anglican and a Lutheran or Calvinist; politically it would give protestantism a position in the Holy Land, but ecclesiologically it was anathema to the Tractarians. Newman's only defence of the Church of England now was that it still had the apostolic succession and the creed, as well as the ecclesiological note of holiness.

The development of doctrine

Newman's parish of St Mary's included the village of Littlemore, 2 miles outside Oxford, where Newman had had a church—also St Mary's—built in 1836. In February 1842 he moved out to a row of cottages nearby which he had leased. Not only did he want to get away from controversy in Oxford but since 1840 he had been seriously thinking of trying to found some kind of monastic or religious community, if only because he felt that the lack of religious life in the Church of England would drive the younger, more advanced Tractarians into the arms of Rome. His own objections to Rome were somewhat shaken at the end of 1842, when Charles Russell, a professor at the seminary in Maynooth, sent him an English translation of some unexceptionable sermons by the Neapolitan St Alphonsus Liguori, where, if anywhere, one might have expected to find the kind of extreme Mariolatry that was assumed to be part of the popular Catholicism or popery that Newman had denounced. He did find that some passages on the Virgin Mary had been omitted as unsuitable for English-speaking readers, but this seemed to show that there was a devotional pluralism in the Roman church. In December 1842 he sent a retraction of his more extreme anti-Roman statements to an Oxford newspaper.

On 2 February 1843 Newman preached the last of his Oxford University sermons (published under that title in the same month), 'The theory of developments in religious doctrine'. His argument that the apostolic church had an implicit if not an explicit knowledge of later doctrinal formulations relied upon key ideas he had worked out in the six sermons on the relation between faith and reason which he had preached between 1839 and 1841. Newman defined faith as the kind of implicit rather than explicit reasoning which depends not on evidences but on 'antecedent probabilities' or presumptions, which in the case of religion would be

determined by one's moral dispositions. The originality
of these sermons lay in their refusal to assume the
Enlightenment's opposition of faith and reason and to
abandon (like Schleiermacher) religion's claim to truth by
conceding to science all factual knowledge and claiming
for religious statements merely emotional, imaginative,
and existential significance. Instead, Newman defined
faith in terms of a wider concept of reasoning than had
been current since the seventeenth century. The
epistemology of these sermons, the most seminal of his
writings, contained the seeds of his later educational and
philosophical thought.

Early in September 1843 Newman resigned as vicar of
St Mary's, believing that he no longer had the confidence
of the bishops and feeling less and less confident himself
about his own position in the Church of England. On the
25th he preached at Littlemore his last sermon as an
Anglican, 'The parting of friends', taking as his text the
same verse of the Psalms which he had taken for the first
sermon he ever wrote: 'Man goes forth to his work and to
his labour until the evening.'

Not only was Newman's own position becoming more
and more untenable, but the movement itself seemed to
have a momentum which led irresistibly towards Rome. In
December 1843 Newman decided to discontinue the series
of lives of the English saints which he had begun editing,
as it was impossible to write sympathetically about pre-

Reformation saints without betraying a sympathy for
things Roman Catholic. His conviction that the Church of
England was in schism was now greater than his belief that
certain Roman Catholic dogmas were not true
developments of the original revelation. In the course of
1844 he revealed to friends that he was on the verge of
joining the Roman Catholic Church; holding the
convictions that he did, he now needed only to be certain
that he was not under some delusion. At the end of 1844 he
resolved to write a book on the question of doctrinal
development, and to seek admission to the Roman Catholic
Church if the writing of the book did not alter his opinions.
In February 1845 the heads of the Oxford colleges voted to
permit convocation to vote on a censure of Tract 90. Only
the intervention of R. W. Church, the senior proctor,
prevented, by a procedural device, this vote.

The Essay on Development and reception
into the Catholic church

Newman began to send instalments of the *Essay on the
Development of Christian Doctrine* to the printers in late
September 1845. It was never properly completed
(though it was published that year), as the author had
decided to become a Roman Catholic on the strength of
the argument already advanced and felt there was no
more to be said. His thesis was that since a living idea is
necessarily a developing idea, and development brings

out rather than obscures the original idea, doctrinal development is to be expected and indeed welcomed in Christianity. But if so, then an infallible authority is needed to distinguish true from false developments in the unfolding of a revelation that claims to be objectively true. Catholicism is the only form of Christianity that shows a continual development that purports to be guaranteed by authority, and modern Catholicism seemed ostensibly to be the historical continuation of early Christianity. Nevertheless Newman proposed, albeit tentatively, seven notes to distinguish authentic developments from corruptions: an idea has not been corrupted. If it retains one and the same type, the same principles, the same organization; if its beginnings anticipate its subsequent phases, and its later phenomena protect and subserve its earlier; if it has a power of assimilation and revival, and a vigorous action from first to last. (*Essay on the Development of Christian Doctrine*)

The *Essay on Development* is Newman's best-known theological work and remains the starting point for modern Catholic theology of doctrinal development.

On 3 October 1845 Newman resigned his fellowship at Oriel College. On 9 October he was received into the Roman Catholic Church by Blessed Dominic Barberi, the Italian Passionist missionary. At the end of the month he went to Oscott College, near Birmingham, to be confirmed by Nicholas Wiseman, then president of the college and also coadjutor to the vicar apostolic of the midland district. Wiseman offered Newman and the other converts from the Littlemore community the use of the old Oscott College (renamed Maryvale by Newman). Newman stayed there from February to September 1846, when he left for the College of Propaganda in Rome to study for the priesthood.

The Oratory

Dismayed by the state of theology at Rome which preceded the Thomist revival, Newman was also worried by the critical reaction to his *Essay on Development*, which leading theologians felt had gone too far in applying the principle of development. However, Rome gave him the opportunity of visiting the Oratory of St Philip Neri. The idea of founding an Oratory in England had been originally suggested by Wiseman: as a community of secular priests living together under a rule but not vows, the oratory offered a form of religious life without having to join a religious order, as well as the opportunity to combine a pastoral apostolate with educational and intellectual work. Ordained a priest on 30 May 1847, a month later Newman began an Oratorian novitiate in Rome with other members of the Maryvale community. Five months later he was confirmed as superior of the new English Oratory, and on 1 February

1848 the Birmingham Oratory was formally set up at
Maryvale. Two weeks later Newman somewhat reluctantly
admitted to the community F. W. Faber and his Brothers of
the Will of God. Faber, a poet and former fellow of
University College, Oxford, had come over to Rome a few
weeks after Newman, bringing with him a group of young
men from his Anglican parish, who were living in
community with him at St Wilfrid's, Staffordshire.

Newman himself was in the process of publishing
(anonymously) his first novel, *Loss and Gain: the Story of
a Convert*. The book is partly autobiographical, not least
in its preoccupation with finding a real as opposed to
unreal religion. The hero's discovery of the objective
reality of Catholic worship was meant to reflect
Newman's own experience after his conversion,
particularly his fascination with the reservation of the
sacrament making Christ 'really' present in every Catholic
church. The inconsistencies of the comprehensiveness of
the Church of England and of Anglo-Catholicism are
amusingly satirized in what are probably the most
memorable parts of a novel of which the chief claim to
originality lies in the introduction of a new kind of
introspective self-questioning into English fiction.

Maryvale and later St Wilfrid's were intended only as
temporary sites for the new community, and in February
1849 the Oratory was formally set up in a disused gin
distillery in Alcester Street, Birmingham. At the opening

Newman preached a sermon, later published as the first of *Discourses Addressed to Mixed Congregations* (1849), which are more rhetorical than his Anglican sermons, sometimes in a rather Italianate manner. The working-class parishioners were not the educated congregation that was supposed to be the object of the new English Oratory's apostolate, and London would obviously have been a more suitable place, but Newman personally welcomed the opportunity to combine ordinary pastoral with academic and intellectual work. In May the two original communities, which increasingly took different approaches and were too large for a single Oratory, split, and another Oratory was founded under Faber in London. Faber's exuberant style had already caused Newman problems with a series of translations of continental lives of the saints, the extravagant and even sensational character of which had offended 'old Catholics', including W. B. Ullathorne, the new vicar apostolic, who had succeeded Wiseman after the latter's appointment to London.

At the invitation of the London oratorians, Newman in the summer of 1850 delivered *Lectures on Certain Difficulties Felt by Anglicans in Submitting to the Catholic Church*. They were a response to the privy council's decision in the Gorham case that baptismal regeneration was not an essential doctrine of the Church of England, which caused a crisis for Anglo-Catholics

and brought many over to Rome, including the future
Cardinal Manning. Urging, often to great satirical effect,
that common sense shows that Anglo-Catholicism is
inconsistent and unreal, Newman recounted how his own
study of the early church had led him to recognize that
the church of the fathers was identical with the Roman
Catholic Church.

The Catholic years

After the restoration of a Roman Catholic hierarchy to England in September 1850, Wiseman, who had been made a cardinal, issued a triumphalist pastoral letter 'from out the Flaminian gate', which was read out in churches on 20 October. Against this so-called papal aggression a 'no-popery' agitation flared up, and in response Newman delivered another series of lectures in Birmingham in the summer of 1851, published as *Lectures on the Present Position of Catholics in England*. Regarded by Newman as his best-written book (it contains his best satire), it aimed to reveal the inconsistencies and the unreality of the powerful British anti-Catholic tradition. One fifth of the lectures contained a denunciation of Giacinto Achilli, a former Dominican priest who had become a protestant after being found guilty of sexual assault. Brought to England in 1850 by the Evangelical Alliance, he had toured the country speaking to packed audiences. Relying on the information in Wiseman's published (but anonymous) indictment of Achilli, Newman had been advised that libel proceedings were highly unlikely as no action had been taken against Wiseman, who would easily be able to prove his

allegations. In November 1851 Achilli denied on oath all
the charges against him, an affidavit which enabled him
to institute criminal rather than civil proceedings against
Newman. Unfortunately, not only had Wiseman mislaid
the crucial documentary evidence which would have
stopped the case, but he failed to enable the two
Birmingham Oratorians who had gone to Italy to obtain
the evidence they needed. The necessary documents and
evidence were found too late to prevent Newman from
being committed to trial on a criminal charge for which
he was liable to a year's imprisonment.

The Catholic University of Ireland

Newman was not only busy with the preparations for the
new Oratory House that was being built in Edgbaston but
was also preoccupied with the establishment of a new
Catholic university in Ireland. In April 1851 Paul Cullen,
then archbishop of Armagh and afterwards of Dublin, had
asked him for his advice and also to give some lectures.
After the majority of Irish bishops had refused to support
the new non-denominational Queen's Colleges, Rome
had urged them to set up a Catholic university on the lines
of the University of Louvain in Belgium. In November
the organizing committee, headed by Cullen, appointed
Newman the first president. In May and June 1852
Newman delivered five of the *Discourses on the Scope*

Scope and Nature of University Education (1852), which became the first half of *The Idea of a University* (1873).

In these classic lectures Newman defended the idea of a liberal education within a confessional religious context against both utilitarian attacks and anti-intellectual clericalism. The skilful rhetoric contrived to do justice to the complexities of the Irish situation, as well as to argue for the central place of theology among the branches of knowledge, but without detriment to the ideal of a liberal education, which for Newman meant essentially an intellectual training of the whole mind. The *Lectures and Essays on University Subjects* (1859), a collection of addresses and papers delivered and written while Newman was rector of the university, and which later became the second half of *The Idea of a University*, offered specific application of the more theoretical ideas of the first part, particularly in arguing that there need be no conflict between theology and science, which should respect each other as different ways of understanding the world.

The Achilli trial took place at the end of June 1852, when the jury decided that Newman had been unable to prove all his charges, which was practically impossible. Still, he had won a moral victory, and *The Times* in a leading article commented that Catholics could not expect justice in a British court. In January 1853 the prejudice of the jury was implicitly acknowledged by the judge, who let Newman off with a fine of £100. In July 1852 he had celebrated the revival of Catholicism in his famous sermon 'The second spring', which was delivered at the first provincial synod of the new ecclesiastical hierarchy held at Oscott—when, however, he warned that it might turn out to be like an uncertain English spring.

It was not until October 1853 that Newman received from the university committee a mandate to start the university. But during October and November he was already engaged to give a course of lectures in Liverpool, published as *Lectures on the History of the Turks in its Relation to Christianity* (1854), which were delivered against the background of hostilities between Orthodox Russia and Muslim Turkey. In January 1854, much to Newman's disapproval, Britain and France became involved on the side of Turkey in what soon became the Crimean War. In March Newman began sending a series of letters, 'Who's to blame?', to the *Catholic Standard*, which contained his first real foray into political theory.

Newman had as yet received no official recognition from the Irish bishops, who were divided about the feasibility of the university and suspected Cullen of wanting sole control over it. Wiseman's idea of Newman's being made a titular bishop to give him more authority was scotched by last-minute reservations on the part of Cullen. In February 1854 Newman arrived in Ireland to consult and take soundings, as well as to advertise the university. He found a distinct lack of enthusiasm, not only among some of the bishops but particularly among the educated Catholic laity, who saw no need for a Catholic, let alone a clerical, university in the denominationally mixed community of Ireland. Irish nationalists like Archbishop MacHale of Tuam were also hostile to any English involvement. It was not until May 1854 that the bishops formally approved the university's statutes and the appointment of Newman as rector. Newman immediately began a weekly *Catholic University Gazette*, in which during 1854 he published a series of articles, later collected as *Office and Work of Universities* (1856). These developed his educational thought, not least his emphasis on the importance of the student–teacher relationship, as well as his ideal of a university which would combine the college tutorial principle of Oxford with the university professorial system of a continental university like Louvain, where the rector and professors rather than heads of colleges governed the university. On 3 November 1854 the university opened with about twenty students in residence and another forty expected.

At the end of July 1855 Newman resumed work on a second novel, begun in 1848. *Callista* (1856) remains interesting as an imaginative attempt to recreate the world of the primitive church—in this case third-century Africa—where an analogy between the situation of the early Christians facing persecution in the Roman empire and that of Catholics in nineteenth-century Britain is clearly intended to strike the reader. But it is also a much more profound exploration of the process of conversion (here from unbelief to Christian faith) than that of his earlier *Loss and Gain*, as well as containing a strikingly existential theology of hell.

In October 1855 a long and bitter dispute between the Birmingham and London Oratories began. Ostensibly, it was over the latter's successful application to Rome for a dispensation from the clause in the Oratorian rule, adapted by Newman for England, which forbade the spiritual direction of nuns. Newman felt he had not been properly consulted, and the Birmingham Oratory resented the fact that when the dispensation came in November it seemed to be intended for both Oratories. There were two connected reasons why an apparently trivial difference turned into such a deep alienation: almost from the beginning not only had there been inevitable tensions between two communities under two such different superiors but a disagreement about the nature of the Oratory itself had emerged, with Newman insisting on the intellectual apostolate and Faber on the exclusively spiritual and devotional mission of the Oratory. Faber and his companions had moved to London, which meant that their Oratory was now in a much more prominent situation than the mother house and potentially in a position to dictate to the Birmingham house. Although

Oratories were meant to be autonomous and independent, there was nevertheless a common rule governing the two Oratories, for which Newman as the founder of the English Oratory was responsible, so that any dispensation or ruling from Rome inevitably affected both houses. Anxious to ensure that no ruling from Rome to one of the English Oratories should be binding on the other, and that no interpretation of the rule should be made by one Oratory without the other's knowing, Newman set off at the end of December 1855 for Rome, where he had a satisfactory audience with Pope Pius IX. The final, formal separation of the Oratories took place with the London Oratory's successful application in the summer of 1856 for a separate foundation brief.

In May 1856 a university church was opened on ground next to the University House in St Stephen's Green in Dublin. Newman had from the beginning hoped to found an Oratory which would provide chaplains for the university. The university sermons he preached there were published in *Sermons Preached on Various Occasions* (1857), in which a principal theme is the importance of Christian humanism combining the religious and the intellectual which, he thought, had characterized St Philip Neri and the Oratory from the beginning.

In spite of the difficulty of finding students because of the low level of secondary education in Ireland and the failure of those Irish and English Catholics who could afford to do so to support the university, the project was not a complete failure: the medical school was a success as was the launch of an academic journal entitled *The Atlantis*. Newman's official leave of absence from the Birmingham Oratory expired in 1857, when he sent his resignation to the Irish bishops. He felt it was impossible to be both provost of the Birmingham Oratory and rector of the university, and indeed his absences during vacations were a constant source of tension between him and Cullen. But there were other serious disagreements: Cullen wanted the kind of discipline that would have been appropriate for a seminary; Newman thought that he should be allowed to appoint the vice-rector; and most significant of all, Cullen refused to countenance a lay finance committee and strongly disapproved of Newman's appointment of laymen, including leading Irish nationalists, to chairs. Newman agreed to stay on temporarily as part-time rector, but finally resigned in 1858. In retrospect he thought he had been wrong not to have insisted on certain conditions before accepting the rectorship. He also considered the pope ill-advised to have tried to found a Catholic university in Ireland.

The laity

Newman realized that the tensions between laity and clergy, which had hampered his efforts in Dublin, were not peculiar to Ireland, but were a feature of the increasingly ultramontane nineteenth-century church. In March 1859 he reluctantly agreed to take on temporarily the editorship of the popular liberal Catholic magazine *The Rambler*, which was threatened by ecclesiastical censure, as the only person acceptable to the bishops on the one hand and the editor, Richard Simpson, and the chief proprietor, Sir John Acton, on the other. Newman fully supported a lay Catholic magazine concerned to encourage the intellectual life of Catholics, but disapproved of its critical attitude towards authority and of theological articles by untrained laymen. In May he received a letter of complaint from John Gillow, a professor of theology at Ushaw seminary, about a passage which Newman had written in the May issue upholding the right of lay Catholics to express their views on matters which concerned them, such as educational standards in Catholic schools. Gillow had particularly complained about Newman's pointing out that the laity had even been consulted before the definition of the immaculate conception in 1854. Newman's point, however, was not that their opinion had been sought but that the fact of their faith had been ascertained. On the advice of his bishop, he decided to resign after the July number, in which he set out a scholarly and theological defence of the role of the laity in the famous article 'On consulting the faithful in matters of doctrine'. His first point was that 'consulting' was used in the sense in which a doctor consults the pulse of his patient and not that in which the patient consults the doctor. The laity's faith was important because the *consensus fidelium* witnessed to the tradition of the church, as during the Arian heresy in the fourth century when the laity was more faithful than the episcopate in witnessing to the doctrine of the divinity of Christ.

Gillow again wrote to complain that Newman appeared to be denying the church's infallibility. Newman replied that he had admitted only a temporary suspension of function on the part of the teaching authority at the time. An official complaint was made to Rome by Bishop Brown of Newport. At the request of Bishop Ullathorne, Newman wrote to Wiseman to say that he was ready to comply with any demands the Holy See might make. The list of objectionable passages drawn up by the Congregatio de Propaganda Fide (under which England, as a quasi-missionary country, came) was never forwarded by Wiseman (then a sick man) to Newman, who assumed the matter was closed. The Roman authorities, on the other hand, assumed that Newman's failure to offer an explanation proved his disobedience.

Newman's Apologia

The disappointments and setbacks of the past decade had taken their toll on Newman, and in the summer of 1861 he was advised by his doctor to rest for several months.

Not only was he exhausted but he was deeply depressed. After all his trials as an Anglican, his Catholic life seemed to be almost uniformly unsuccessful. Apart from the Irish university and *The Rambler*, there had been the abortive affair of the translation of the Bible, with which he had been entrusted by the English bishops in 1855— although Wiseman did not see fit to inform him officially until 1857. He had agreed to undertake a work that was hardly congenial to him, and made preliminary preparations; but after a request from the American bishops to co-operate in a joint translation, he never heard any more about the project from the English hierarchy. Ever anxious to encourage Catholic education, he had responded to the need for a new type of Catholic school, which would provide the kind of education that the public schools offered and that the middle-class converts particularly wanted for their children, by opening the Oratory School in 1859. Faber's disapproval of the undertaking as un-oratorian influenced Wiseman, who had taken the London Oratory's side in the quarrel with Birmingham, and the school was also resented by the existing Catholic schools which were run on very different lines.

On 30 December 1863 Newman was sent anonymously a copy of the January number of *Macmillan's Magazine*, containing a review by the Revd Charles Kingsley (1819–1875), a successful novelist and regius professor of

modern history at Cambridge, in which he accused
Newman in particular, and the Roman Catholic Church in
general, of preferring cunning to truth. The ensuing
correspondence with the publisher and Kingsley was
published by Newman as a satirical pamphlet in February
1864 and elicited a highly favourable review by the
literary critic R. H. Hutton, who scornfully dismissed
Kingsley's pamphlet of rejoinder. Long used to aspersions
on his integrity, Newman now decided to take advantage
of an attack by such a well-known public figure to write
an apologia for his conversion, which would finally
convince the protestant public that he had not been an
agent for popery as a Tractarian and that his submission to
Rome was entirely sincere. The resulting classic
autobiography—more theological than spiritual—
appeared in weekly pamphlets to take advantage of the
publicity aroused by the controversy. The pressure was
enormous, but Newman shared the strain of remembering
the Oxford Movement with old Anglican friends, who lent
him letters and offered advice and criticism. The
pamphlets were published as a volume in 1864 entitled
Apologia pro vita sua. In the last chapter Newman
undertook a general defence of Catholicism, particularly
the infallibility of the church, which he directed not only
at protestants and sceptics, but also more covertly at
Catholic ultramontanes or extreme papalists, against
whom he urged a balanced theology of authority and

freedom, in which the interaction, even conflict, of the magisterium and the theologians was depicted as creative and necessary for the life of the church. It was his second significant contribution to a theology of the church.

Against the ultramontanes

Not only was the *Apologia* a best-seller, making Newman financially secure for the first time since he became a Catholic, but the reviews were almost universally favourable, especially the nonconformist ones, and there was no doubt about the support of the vast majority of the Catholic clergy. It was a turning point, and Newman's depression lifted. Nor did it return when his next project, the possibility of founding an Oratory in Oxford, was foiled. When in August 1864 he was offered the chance of buying a 5 acre plot of ground, he was asked by Bishop Ullathorne to establish a church and mission in Oxford. Ullathorne made it clear that he would not countenance a Catholic college being built, as had been mooted by the original buyer. The idea of an apostolate to the Catholic undergraduates who were already at Oxford appealed to Newman. News of the possibility alerted the English ultramontanes, and H. E. Manning, who was now Wiseman's closest aide, obtained an instruction from Rome to the English bishops to hold an extraordinary meeting, as a result of which Catholics were formally warned against attending protestant universities—an inevitable pronouncement given the official Catholic opposition to 'mixed' education. Newman was convinced that the ultramontanes' real fear was not that the faith of Catholic undergraduates would be undermined, but that he, Newman, would be able to exert an important influence in forming an educated laity. Newman sold the land, but bought a smaller plot in case the situation should change.

In the summer of 1865 Newman published in the Catholic periodical *The Month* his poem *The Dream of Gerontius*. In the depths of his depression he had seriously thought he might be about to die, and it seems to have been this prospect of death which led to his writing the poem later made famous in Edward Elgar's oratorio. The verses 'Praise to the Holiest in the height' became one of the most famous hymns in the English language. The poem contained, like the treatment of hell in *Callista*, a deeply spiritual depiction of purgatory, very different from the conventional one of a place of physical punishment. Another controversial work followed in January 1866: the publication of E. B. Pusey's *Eirenicon* in 1865, in answer to Manning's pamphlet of 1864 (ostensibly attacking Pusey but also implicitly criticizing the *Apologia*), led to Newman's writing his *Letter to Pusey*. While complaining about the contradiction between Pusey's professed desire for Christian unity and his provocative citation of extreme Marian devotions in the Roman Catholic Church as though they were obligatory or typical, Newman took the opportunity to dissociate himself from the devotionalism of Faber as well as the ultramontanism of converts such as Manning (who had succeeded Wiseman as archbishop of Westminster) and W. G. Ward, the lay editor of the *Dublin Review*. Apart from pointing out that Catholic Mariology was essentially the same as that of the fathers and that the Virgin Mary's intercessory role was quite distinct from actual invocation of her, Newman also observed that a popular religion like Catholicism was inevitably open to abuse and corruption, a point which represented a further stage in his developing ecclesiology.

After yet another request from Bishop Ullathorne to undertake the Oxford mission, the Birmingham Oratory in April 1866 conditionally agreed to build a church on the smaller plot of land for which it would provide a priest. Ullathorne assured a somewhat reluctant Newman, who was adamant that his only motive in becoming involved was to look after Catholic undergraduates, that the policy of discouraging rather than forbidding Catholics from going to Oxford would continue unless there were a substantial increase in numbers. At the end of the year Ullathorne told Newman that permission had been given by Rome for an Oxford Oratory, but concealed the directive that Newman himself was not to reside there lest his presence should encourage Catholics to send their sons to Oxford.

Donations had already begun coming in when, in March 1867, the Congregatio de Propaganda Fide complained that it had received a report that the Oratory School was actively preparing boys to go to Oxford. In fact it was doing no more than other Catholic schools, but the complaint meant that the school would have to discontinue the special tuition needed. The letter from Rome was the result of English ultramontane dismay that permission for an Oxford Oratory had been given. Then in April a report appeared in an English Catholic newspaper to the effect that the pope had decided that Newman was too theologically unsound to be allowed to go to Oxford. The bishop now revealed the instruction which he had suppressed on the ground that it concerned an eventuality which had not been contemplated. However, the newspaper report provoked a published protest signed by many prominent lay Catholics in favour of Newman. His closest confidant at the oratory, Ambrose St John, went to Rome to defend both the school, of which he was in charge, and Newman himself. There he found that the authorities still held *The Rambler* article against Newman, who had apparently never answered the charges against it, but were otherwise interested only in maintaining the official policy against 'mixed' education; personal hostility to Newman and what he stood for seems to have been confined to the English ultramontanes. After Propaganda Fide, at the instigation of Manning, had ordered the English bishops to issue a much stronger prohibition against Catholics attending non-Catholic universities, Newman formally resigned the Oxford mission.

For years now Newman had been trying to work out a philosophy of faith in the face of the growing de-Christianization of modern society. In his *Oxford University Sermons* he had argued that religious belief involved the same kind of informal reasoning that was unhesitatingly employed in other areas without accusations of irrationality. The problem still remained as to whether one could talk of attaining certitude, when the kind of certainty involved was clearly so different from the objective certainty of logically necessary propositions and empirically verifiable factual statements. At last in August 1866, while on holiday in Switzerland, he decided that he had been wrong to start from the problem of certitude, since certitude was a kind of assent, which in turn must be distinguished from inference. The discovery was the beginning of nearly four years of strenuous work on *An Essay in Aid of a Grammar of Assent* (1870).

Newman began by distinguishing between the assent one makes to a proposition and the conclusion one draws from an inference, arguing that assenting and inferring were two distinct kinds of activity. Assent might be 'notional' or 'real', depending on whether one's apprehension of a proposition was notional or real. Newman's usage can be confusing because, although 'notional' seems to mean what is abstract or general, and 'real' what is concrete and individual, nevertheless the distinction is not in fact between sense perceptions and mental abstractions but between experiential and non-experiential knowledge. Thus a mental act may bring before the mind a more vivid image than a sensible object. Newman argued that conscience can suggest the existence of God if intimations of conscience are seen as the echoes of a magisterial voice suggestive of a God of whom we gain a real image from, and in, these dictates of conscience. Arguing that, where formal logical inference is impossible, it is the cumulation of probabilities which leads to certainty, Newman pointed out that assent to the truth of non-logical propositions involves personal judgement. This judgement, similar to Aristotle's *phronesis*, Newman called the 'illative sense', which operates more or less implicitly and instinctively, without formal verbal analysis.

Written by a disciple of the Anglican philosopher of religion Bishop Joseph Butler from within a pragmatic philosophical tradition, the *Grammar of Assent* inevitably found little favour with Catholic scholastic philosophers. Well aware that the alleged weakness of the work was its failure to provide a criterion of certainty, Newman's originality lay in recognizing that the truths in question were not empirically or logically demonstrable.

Papal infallibility

In June 1867 the pope announced that a general council was to be held. Newman was immediately alarmed that the ultramontanes would press for a definition of papal infallibility. But he refused three invitations, including one from Pope Pius IX himself, to attend as a theological consultor on the grounds that he had no aptitude for committee work nor the kind of professional expertise that would be needed. In January 1870 he received a letter from Bishop Ullathorne deploring the way in which the ultramontanes were lobbying for a definition. Newman thought a definition was uncalled for, as there was no heresy threatening papal authority, and also dangerous, because there had not been sufficient preparation and study to justify such a sudden and unnecessary development. Newman's extremely strong response to the bishop was leaked to the newspapers. In fact, the actual definition that was passed by the majority of the bishops in July 1870 struck Newman as so moderate as to constitute a defeat for the ultramontanes.

The loss of Rome by the pope in September 1870 meant the end of the Papal States and of his temporal power, about which Newman, to the annoyance of the English ultramontanes, had been less than enthusiastic.

Perhaps his new spiritual powers—which Newman thought popes had acted on in practice for at least 300 years—were after all providential: at least they would give the church an enhanced central authority against attempts by the state to control local churches. Still, Newman knew only too well that the definition would cause a lot of problems for Catholics, particularly in protestant countries. History, however, seemed to show that declarations of councils were modified in the sense of being qualified and complemented by later councils.

In November 1874 W. E. Gladstone—influenced by the excommunicated German Catholic church historian J. J. I. von Döllinger—published a best-selling pamphlet alleging that the infallibility definition had not only deprived Catholics of their intellectual freedom but also put their civic loyalty into serious question. Newman saw his opportunity to disown the extreme ultramontanism of Manning, which had partly inspired Gladstone's outburst. The resulting *Letter to the Duke of Norfolk* (the leading Catholic layman), which was actually, like the *Letter to Pusey*, a short book, was published in January 1875. In it Newman pointed out that all doctrinal pronouncements of councils and popes required the interpretation of theologians, just as the meaning of the laws of the legislature had to be determined by lawyers. Moreover, magisterial definitions of an abstract nature had to be applied to concrete situations and to admit of exceptions.

Theology, too, had its own principles and rules, not least that of minimizing the force and scope of a teaching, which were an important part of the church's tradition. The most famous part of the *Letter* was Newman's raising of a toast to 'the pope if you please—still to conscience first, and to the pope afterwards' (*Letter to Pusey*). Newman admitted the possibility of conscientious disobedience to a papal edict, but not to a papal teaching, which, since it had to be of a general nature, could not represent a practical dictate to the individual.

Last years

Although the *Letter to the Duke of Norfolk* was Newman's last book, it was not his last word on ecclesiology. In 1877, as part of the process of republishing his Anglican and Catholic writings in a uniform series, he added a lengthy preface to the *Lectures on the Prophetical Office*. In his *Essay on Development*, which he was to reissue in a greatly revised edition in 1878, he had argued that the dogmas of Catholicism were not corruptions but developments of the original revelation. In the 1877 preface he maintained that the superstitions and abuses of power to be found in the history of the Catholic church were not corruptions of its theology (which would be rationalism), but of the church's other two 'offices', namely its worship and government. The anomalies to be found in Catholicism resulted from the church's difficulty in combining all three offices at the same time, and while Newman saw theology as predominant, since without its subject matter, revelation, the church would not be a political power or a religious rite, nevertheless he allowed that at times theology had to take into account and respect the devotions of popular religion and also even 'political' considerations, as the church is the church militant as well.

In May 1877 Newman was sent one of the three drawings made of him by a friend, Lady Coleridge. As well as the famous voice, people who met him for the first time were particularly struck by his strangely mysterious expression, which was evidently evoked better in her portraits than in others (including that painted by J. E. Millais c.1881). Unlike W. T. Roden's portrait (1874?), which emphasized Newman's keen sensitivity, Lady Coleridge succeeded in integrating it with the resoluteness and strength that also marked his character.

In December 1877 Newman received a surprise invitation from Trinity College, Oxford, to become its first honorary fellow, an honour which he deeply appreciated, particularly as his memories of Trinity were happier than those of Oriel—as he had indicated in the famous account in the *Apologia* of his taking leave of Oxford in 1846. This was followed by an even greater honour in 1879, when he was made a cardinal by the new, more liberal Pope Leo XIII. Although such a dignity seemed quite alien to him, he felt that he had no alternative but to accept the red hat: not only would it end all suspicions of his orthodoxy and his commitment to the Catholic church but it would also signify that ultramontanism was not the only acceptable kind of Catholicism and would mark the beginning of a new openness in Rome, as the pope intended. In his *biglietto* speech, Newman adverted to the significance of his elevation, while at the same time affirming his lifelong opposition to that liberalism which rejects dogma and the objectivity of religious truth.

In 1881 Select *Treatises of St Athanasius* was published in two volumes, a greatly revised and altered version of the edition Newman had contributed to the Tractarian Library of the Fathers, which completed the uniform edition of the works. But it was not the last of his publications. In 1882 he published, with a preface, *Notes of a Visit to the Russian Church in the Years 1840, 1841*, which had been compiled by William Palmer while he was a Tractarian fellow of Magdalen; Palmer had recently died after becoming a Catholic. Then in 1884 Newman published an article in *Nineteenth Century* on the problem of the inspiration of scripture, which was more sophisticated than the prevailing Catholic theory of the time in arguing that it was the biblical writers, not the writings themselves, who were directly inspired. And finally, in October 1885, in an article in the *Contemporary Review*, he defended himself against the frequent charge of scepticism which was made against him, later to be put forward with force by Leslie Stephen in 'Cardinal Newman's scepticism' (*Nineteenth Century*, Feb 1891), in emphasizing conscience and imagination in religious belief rather than so-called reason.

From the latter half of 1886 Newman's health began to fail, and he celebrated mass for the last time on Christmas day 1889. On 11 August 1890 he died of pneumonia at the Birmingham Oratory. He was buried on the 19th in the grave of Ambrose St John at the Oratory country house at Rednal, outside Birmingham. The pall over the coffin bore his cardinal's motto *Cor ad cor loquitur* ('Heart speaks to heart'). On his memorial tablet were inscribed the words he had chosen: *Ex umbris et imaginibus in veritatem* ('Out of shadows and phantasms into the truth').

Beatification

The Cause

During Newman's lifetime there were many who regarded him as a saint. Father Bernard Dalgairns, to take a particularly significant example, who was a disloyal member of the Birmingham Oratory and a particular thorn in Newman's side, reported to Father Faber his final interview with Newman before departing to join the rival London Oratory: 'His eyes looked then just like a Saint's and he spoke and acted like one, so disinterestedly, so gently.' At Newman's death the ultra-Protestant *Evangelical Magazine* declared that of all the saints 'in the Roman calendar there are very few that can be considered better entitled to that designation than Cardinal Newman'. However, the Birmingham Oratory, bearing in mind the dictum of St. Philip Neri, 'to love to be unknown', that was so dear to Newman himself, refused to push his Cause. And it was not until 1941 that an American Dominican, Fr Charles Callan, called for the Cause to be opened in an article in *America* magazine. Then in 1942 the Archbishop of Toronto, in response to the overwhelmingly positive response, gave his imprimatur to the first prayer for Newman's for

Newman's canonisation. Finally, in England itself the Newman scholar Mgr. H. Francis Davis gave his support in an article in 1952. Six years later the Archbishop of Birmingham opened the Cause, and a year later set up a historical commission to examine the evidence. However, it was not until 1986 that a reconstituted historical commission completed the necessary documentation to conclude the diocesan process. This was then sent to Rome to the Congregation for the Causes of Saints, which subsequently confirmed the conclusion reached by the commission. Accordingly, on 22 January 1991, Pope John Paul II declared Newman to be 'Venerable' or a figure to be venerated for the 'heroic virtues' that he displayed in his life. The formal recognition by the pope of Newman as 'Venerable' still required divine confirmation in order for him to reach the next rung, so to speak, in the ladder to sainthood, that of beatification.

Although there had never, not surprisingly, been the kind of popular cult of Newman the theologian and writer that a figure like Mother Teresa inspired with her obvious works of heroic charity, over the years the belief that Newman was a saint had been growing all over the Catholic world. As a result, more and more people were praying for his intercession. And then on 15 August 2001, the feast of the Assumption of the Blessed Virgin Mary, an American living in Marshfield near Boston, who was training for the married diaconate, was inexplicably cured of a severe spinal disorder that had left him bent doubled over. Jack Sullivan claimed it was the result of his seeking in prayer the intercession of Newman, ever since watching a television interview with the present winter a year previously in June 2000. Thereupon the archdiocese of Boston established a tribunal that interviewed witnesses and collected all the evidence available, which was then forwarded to the Congregation for the Causes of Saints in Rome in November 2006. On 24 April 2008 the medical consultants at the Congregation unanimously agreed that they could not find any natural explanation for the cure. Then on 23 April 2009 the Congregation's theological consultants unanimously recognized Jack Sullivan's recovery as a miracle. Following these two decisions, Pope Benedict XVI decreed on 3 July 2009 that Newman be beatified. On 19 September 2010 he will personally beatify Newman at Coventry airport during his visit to England.

In clear anticipation of the beatification, the Congregation for Saints had already instructed that Newman's remains should be exhumed, to allow for their public veneration in accordance with usual Catholic practice. It was then discovered that Newman had been buried in a wooden coffin that, along with his remains, had entirely decomposed in the damp soil, apart from a brass plate (with his name and date of death), the brass handles with some bits of cloth attached, a brass replica of his cardinal's hat, and a wooden crucifix inlaid in silver. This discovery had no implications for the beatification, only for the projected public veneration. One is tempted to feel that Newman's 'disappearance' from this earth was his final fulfilment of the maxim of St. Philip Neri, the founder of the Congregation of the Oratory, which he so cherished: 'amare nesciri', 'to love not to be known'. Indeed, the 20 August 1890 report in *The Birmingham Daily Post* of Newman's funeral and burial ended: 'and then the coffin was covered with mould of a softer texture than the marly [clay and lime] stratum in which the grave is cut. This was done in studious and affectionate fulfilment of a desire of Dr Newman's which some may deem fanciful, but which sprang from his reverence for the letter of the Divine Word; which, as he conceived, enjoins us to facilitate rather than impede the operation of the law "Dust thou art, and unto dust shalt thou return."'

When it became generally known that Newman had been buried, in accordance with his strict instructions, in the same grave as his faithful friend and collaborator, Father Ambrose St. John, there was widespread speculation in the international media that there might have been some kind of homosexual relationship between the two friends. In an age that has almost lost the concept of affectionate friendship untouched by sexual attraction, such speculation was no doubt inevitable. Certainly, the assumption that the desire to be buried in the same grave as someone else may, if not must, indicate some sort of sexual attraction would have greatly astonished previous generations. G.K. Chesterton's devoted secretary, Dorothy Collins, whom he and his wife regarded as a daughter, while thinking it presumptuous to ask to be buried in the same grave as the Chestertons, nevertheless directed that she be cremated and her ashes buried in the same grave. C.S. Lewis and his brother Warnie are buried in the same grave in accordance with both brothers' wishes. For Newman, Ambrose St. John, a fellow priest of the Birmingham Oratory, was the equivalent of a brother: for thirty years he had been his most faithful and loyal supporter, from the days of his virtual exile at Littlemore through all his trials and tribulations as a Catholic. The last work that Newman had asked him to undertake was to translate the Austrian theologian Joseph Fessler's important book on infallibility in the wake of the First Vatican Council, a labour of love that Newman felt had proved too much for his already overworked friend. There was nothing more natural – then at least - than that Newman should want humbly to show his gratitude by directing that he, a famous cardinal, should be buried in the same grave as that of a comparatively unknown priest, his faithful friend and collaborator.

There were, however, almost certainly two other reasons why Newman was so insistent on the place of his burial. First, he must have feared that as a cardinal, and therefore 'prince of the Church', his Oratorian community, or for that matter the Church authorities, might wish to erect the kind of tomb that would normally have been erected for a cardinal, almost certainly away from the privacy of the community cemetery in what was then countryside and in a prominent public place in the Oratory church in Edgbaston, Birmingham. And second, by being buried in the same grave as St. John, between the graves of Joseph Gordon and Edward Caswall, he would lie among the three men 'who in past years gave themselves up to me generously and unreservedly' and who had been 'the life and centre of the Oratory'. After Caswall died and was buried in a grave next to St. John's, Newman had written sadly: 'So now the three most energetic and influential of the first Fathers of the Oratory lie together; and the three who from the first threw in their lot with me …' Nothing was more natural than that he, the founder of the Birmingham Oratory, should wish to lie among them.

The publication in 1957, more than fifty years ago, of Newman's *Autobiographical Writings* made available all the evidence necessary to disprove any notion that Newman was homosexual in his inclinations. In December 1816, following his Evangelical conversion in the preceding summer and autumn, we find Newman, aged fifteen, praying in his private journal to be preserved from the temptations that awaited him on his return home from boarding school for the Christmas holidays. The only two temptations he specifically mentions are dances and parties. The implication is clear: there he will meet girls, from whom he is shielded at a boys' boarding school. In a later entry at the end of December, by which time he has returned home, he condemns dances and all parties of this kind, again writing discreetly in Latin, and hopes that his parents will respect his scruples. That he has reached the age of puberty is clear from his references to the sins and temptations of the flesh. Clearly the school holidays presented temptations to an adolescent boy that were not present in a boys' boarding school – provided, of course, the adolescent boy was not homosexually inclined. Had the pious Evangelical Newman been so inclined in the slightest way - and adolescent boys in an all-male boarding school environment are often sexually confused - we would have found him praying fervently for the school holidays and the accompanying release from an all-male society.

The adolescent Newman's disinclination to mingle in young female society was not only out of a fear for his chastity, but also because of a 'deep imagination' that had taken 'possession' of him in the autumn of 1816 that 'it would be the will of God' that he 'should lead a single life'. In the *Apologia*, he explained why he felt this call to celibacy: 'This anticipation, which has held its ground almost continuously ever since, - with the break of a month now and a month then, up to 1829, and, after that date, without any break at all, - was more or less connected in my mind with the notion, that my calling in life would require such a sacrifice as celibacy involved; as, for instance, missionary work among the heathen, to which I had a great drawing for some years. It also strengthened my feeling of separation from the visible world ...' A modern reader should not need to be reminded that in nineteenth-century England homosexuality was illegal and generally considered to be immoral. The only 'sacrifice' that Newman could possibly be referring to was that of marriage. And he readily acknowledges that from time to time he continued to feel the natural attraction to marriage that any heterosexual man would feel.

Twenty-four years before he wrote those words, he completed on 25 March 1840 his extraordinary account of his near-fatal illness in Sicily in 1833. And, almost bitterly, he counted the cost of the sacrifice he had made in voluntarily embracing celibacy:

The thought keeps pressing on me, while I write this, what am I writing it for? ...

Whom have I, whom can I have, who would take interest in it? ... This is the sort of interest which a wife takes and none but she – it is a woman's interest – and that interest, so be it, shall never be taken in me ... I willingly give up the possession of that sympathy, which I feel is not, cannot be, granted to me. Yet, not the less do I feel the need of it. (*Autobiographical writings*)

These words are unmistakeably the words of a man who feels called to a life of celibacy, while still a clergyman in the Church of England and therefore fully free to get married. But they are also the words of a man who feels the deep pain of sacrificing the love of a woman in marriage.

Certainly, Newman would scarcely have left such an instruction regarding his burial had he even dreamed that it could ever be interpreted as having any significance beyond the significance which he attached to it - nor would the Oratory or the Church authorities have ever permitted such a joint burial if they had had the slightest suspicion about what must have seemed to them a totally innocent, not to say praiseworthy gesture. Newman had plenty of critics, not to say enemies, in his time; yet not one of them, not one newspaper, not one casual observer even dreamed of reading a significance into an act of loving friendship, and indeed of humility, such as was left to the twentieth century to read into it.

A world of Catholic reading
at your fingertips ...

CTS

... now online
Browse 500 titles at

www.cts-online.org.uk

Catholic Faith, Life, and Truth for all